THE ART OF W

NICCOLÒ MACHIAVELLI

THE ART OF WAR

EDITED AND TRANSLATED BY
PETER BONDANELLA AND MARK MUSA

PENGUIN BOOKS

PENGUIN BOOKS

Published by the Penguin Group
Penguin Books Ltd, 27 Wrights Lane, London w8 5tz, England
Penguin Books USA Inc., 375 Hudson Street, New York, New York 10014, USA
Penguin Books Australia Ltd, Ringwood, Victoria, Australia
Penguin Books Canada Ltd, 10 Alcorn Avenue, Toronto, Ontario, Canada m4v 3b2
Penguin Books (NZ) Ltd, 182–190 Wairau Road, Auckland 10, New Zealand

Penguin Books Ltd, Registered Offices: Harmondsworth, Middlesex, England

These selections from *The Art of War* appear in *The Portable
Machiavelli*, edited and translated by Peter Bondanella and
Mark Musa, published in Penguin Books 1979
This edition published 1995
1 3 5 7 9 10 8 6 4 2

Printed in England by Clays Ltd, St Ives plc

CONTENTS

Editors' Note

Many of the general ideas contained in this work on war and military life are essential for an understanding of the most important concepts in Machiavelli's political theory. The Art of War is not without errors of judgment or fundamental conceptual flaws. Machiavelli's distrust of cavalry and his belief in the ineffectiveness of artillery in a modern army led him to make serious tactical blunders and to ignore the actual developments evident in the armies of his own time. His hatred of mercenary troops was motivated more by his humanistic preoccupation with the concept of civic virtue fostered by a citizens' militia than by a reasoned and dispassionate study of the actual military institutions of his day. For example, the armies of Cesare Borgia, which he praised, were composed not of the duke's own subjects, as he imagined, but of professional mercenaries. Moreover, the bloodless battles he described with contempt in several of his works, and which he attributed to the use of mercenary troops, were not, in fact, as bloodless as he imagined. His empirical observations were often distorted by the ideas he discovered in the classical texts on warfare and military leaders by Livy and Tacitus, as well as other writers, and his evaluation of military science in Renaissance Italy was colored by ideological concerns and political preferences. But if his essentially literary and humanistic views hindered an empirical study of military institutions in his time, they also allowed him to envision a more fundamental theoretical relationship between politics and warfare, which resulted in a concept of civic humanism that would be an integral part of the republican legacy in years to come.

The gap between practice and theory in Machiavelli's discussion of the art of war was evident even when the work first appeared in print. In the preface to one of his *Novelle (I, xl)*, Matteo Bandello tells a humorous story about Machiavelli's futile attempts to drill some troops under the command of the brilliant Medici condottiere, Giovanni delle Bande Nere (1494–1526). After more than two hours in the hot Milanese sun, Machiavelli had failed to implement his own advice in the field, yet with only the sound of a drum and the force of his personality the condottiere restored order and corrected Machiavelli's mistakes in the twinkling of an eye. Yet Machiavelli's political duties in the Florentine chancery did provide him with some limited practical military experience, for his first official mission in 1498 involved the war with Pisa. In 1505 he was authorized to raise a body of militiamen from among the Florentine citizenry. His faith in a nonprofessional army was strengthened when his troops took Pisa in 1509. However, his militiamen were no match for the seasoned professional soldiers who attacked Florence in

1512 and restored the Medici to power. His discussion of the essential unity of politics and military science in The Art of War *has always appealed to great military thinkers, including Frederick the Great, Napoleon, and von Clausewitz.*

The Art of War *is divided into a preface and seven books. It is written in the form of a dialogue, a form popular among many humanists of the period, and the discussion of the art of war is set within a conversation among various friends who have gathered, in 1516, at the Orti Oricellari (the gardens belonging to Cosimo Rucellai, a Florentine gentleman) to welcome a well-known mercenary commander, Fabrizio Colonna. After the preface has underlined the essential interdependence of political and military affairs, the succeeding sections of the dialogue deal with: the problems of the citizen soldier (I); arms and military training (II); the role of artillery and the ideal army in battle (III); advice to military leaders (IV); spoils, supplies, and tactics in hostile territory (V); setting up camp, winter campaigns, strategy, and psychological warfare (VI); the defense and siege of cities, rules for war, a portrait of the ideal general, and the hope for a rebirth of ancient military valor in modern Italy (VII). Many of the technical sections will be of interest only to specialists and military historians, but the pages reprinted in this translation—consisting of the complete preface, a major portion of the first book on the citizen soldier, a crucial section from the second book on the relationship of* virtù and Fortuna, *and that part of the seventh book enumerating the qualities of the ideal military leader and calling for a renaissance of classical military skill in modern Italy through an imitation of ancient military institutions— represent fundamental statements that shed light on these and related topics in Machiavelli's major political works. The Art of War was published in 1521, being only one of two works by Machiavelli that appeared in print before his death. It received Renaissance translations into French (1546), English (1563 and 1573), Spanish (1536 and 1541), and German (1623), and continued to be widely read throughout the nineteenth century.*

Preface to The Book of The Art of War
By Niccolò Machiavelli, Citizen
and Florentine Secretary

TO LORENZO DI FILIPPO STROZZI,
FLORENTINE PATRICIAN

Many, Lorenzo, have held and still hold this opinion: that
no two things have less in common or differ more from
each other than a civil and a military life. Hence, one often notices that if a person plans to excel in military life,
he not only immediately changes his way of dressing but
also his habits, his customs, and his voice, thus setting
himself apart from every civilian custom. For he cannot
believe that he who seeks to be ready for any sort of violence can wear civilian clothes; nor can civilian habits and
practices be followed by one who judges these practices to
be effeminate and these customs to be useless to his profession; nor does it appear suitable to retain normal be-
havior and speech when he wishes to terrify other men
with his beard and his curses. This makes such an opinion
in these times seem to be very true.

But if ancient institutions are taken into consideration,
one will find no two things more united, more alike, and,

of necessity, more interrelated than these two; for all of the arts that have been instituted in a civil society for the common good of mankind and all of the institutions established to make men live in fear of the laws and of God would be vain if they were not provided with defenses; such defenses, if they are well organized, will preserve these institutions even if they are poorly organized. And thus, on the contrary, good institutions without military backing undergo the same sort of disorder as do the rooms of a splendid and regal palace which, adorned with gems and gold but lacking a roof, have nothing to protect them from the rain. And if in any other institution of city-states and kingdoms one uses every care to keep men loyal, pacified, and full of the fear of the Lord, in the army this care should really be doubled. For in what man can a country seek greater loyalty than in him who has promised to die for her? In whom should there be more love for peace than in him who can only be harmed by war? In what man should there be more love of God than in him who, submitting himself daily to countless dangers, has more need of His aid? When this necessity was well considered by those who governed empires and were in charge of armies, it caused military life to be praised by other men and to be followed and imitated with great diligence.

But since military institutions are completely corrupted and have, for a long period, diverged from ancient practices, bad opinions about them have arisen, causing the military life to be despised and encouraging men to avoid associating with those who follow this profession. And since I am of the opinion, because of what I have seen and read, that it would not be impossible to restore this profession to ancient methods and to revive in it some measure of its past strength, I have decided, in order to do something of worth and not to waste my leisure time, to write for the satisfaction of those men who love ancient deeds about the art of war as I understand it. And although it is a daring thing to discuss a subject that others have made a profession, nevertheless I do not believe it is wrong to occupy with words a rank which many with greater presumption have held with deeds, for the errors that I commit in writing can be corrected without harm, but those which others have committed in practice cannot be recognized except through the downfall of their governments. Therefore, Lorenzo, please consider the qualities of these labors of mine and, utilizing your judgment, bestow upon them the blame or praise you deem they merit. I send them to you both to show you how grateful I am for the benefits I have received from you—although my capabilities may not equal them—and also because it is the custom to honor with such works those who shine forth in their nobility, their wealth, their intelligence and their generosity—and how well I know that you have few equals in wealth and nobility, fewer still in intelligence, and none in generosity.

Book I

Because I believe that one can praise every man after his death without being blamed, since suspicion of flattery no longer exists, I shall not hesitate to praise our Cosimo Rucellai, whose name I shall never be able to recall to mind without tears, for I recognized in him those qualities desired in a good friend by his friends and in a citizen by his native city. I do not know what he considered to be so much his own (not excepting his soul, to mention nothing else) that he would not spend it willingly for his friends; nor do I know what undertaking would have frightened him if he had perceived the good of his native city in its accomplishment. And I freely confess that I have never met a man, among the many men I have known and have had dealings with, who was more ardent for grandiose and magnificent affairs. Nor did he complain of anything to his friends on his deathbed other than having been born to die young in his home, unhonored, not having been able to assist anyone the way he would have liked to. For he knew that no one could say anything about him other than that a good friend had passed away. Even if his deeds did not materialize, however, that is no reason for us or others who knew him not to bear witness to his praiseworthy qualities. Still, it is true that Fortune was not so completely unfriendly to him that she did not leave some brief reminder of the force of his intelligence, as some of his writings and his love of poetry demonstrate; for although he was not in love, in order not to waste time waiting for Fortune to lead him to higher thoughts he composed such works in his youth. Clearly, from these one can learn with what felicity he expressed his ideas and how greatly he might have been honored in the profession of poetry if he had followed it as his calling. However, since Fortune has deprived us of the presence of such a friend, there appears to be no other remedy than to enjoy his memory as much as possible and to repeat whatever he cleverly stated or wisely argued. And because there is nothing fresher of his memory than the recent conversation he had with Fabrizio Colonna in his gardens (where that captain discussed many affairs of war and Cosimo keenly and wisely addressed many questions to him), it seems fitting to me, since I was present with some of our mutual friends, to preserve it for posterity so that those friends of Cosimo who were also present can, as they read, refresh their memory of his exceptional qualities. Others may lament the fact that they were not present, but they will still learn many things useful not only for military life but also for civilian life, wisely treated by a very intelligent man.

I say, therefore, that when Fabrizio Colonna had returned from Lombardy, where he had fought for some time, with great glory to himself, for the Emperor Charles V, he decided, while passing through Florence, to rest there several days in order to visit His Excellency the Duke of Urbino and to see again several gentlemen with whom he had been friendly in the past. Whereupon Cosimo decided to invite him to his gardens, not so much to demonstrate his generosity as to have cause to speak with him at length, and to hear and learn from him the many things one can hope to learn from such an individual—for Cosimo it represented an opportunity to pass the day discussing those matters which gave his mind the most satisfaction. Fabrizio came, as Cosimo desired, and was received by Cosimo together with several other intimate friends, among whom were Zanobi Buondelmonti, Batista della Palla, and Luigi Alamanni, all young men beloved by him and steeped in the same studies, whose good qualities we shall leave unsaid, for they speak for themselves every day and every hour.

Fabrizio, therefore, was honored (according to the times and the place) by all of them with the greatest possible honors; but when the pleasures of the meal were over and the tables were cleared and all celebrating was done with—something which occurs quickly among great men whose minds are turned toward honorable thoughts—Cosimo, using the pretext of avoiding the heat in order better to satisfy his desire, felt that it was best that they retire to the most private and shaded part of his garden. When they had arrived there and had taken their seats, some on the

7

grass, which is very cool in that place, others upon seats placed in the shadow of the tallest trees, Fabrizio praised the spot as delightful. Looking closely at the trees and not recognizing some of them, he was perplexed. Noticing this, Cosimo said: "Perhaps you do not know some of these trees; but do not be surprised, for there are some here more famous among the ancients than they are among us today." And when he had told him their names and had described how Bernardo, his grandfather, had worked extremely hard in cultivating them, Fabrizio replied: "I had thought as much; this place and this pursuit remind me of several princes of the Kingdom of Naples who delight in these ancient groves and shades."

Pausing at this point in his speech, while sitting pensively there for a moment, he continued: "If I thought I would offend you, I would not give you my opinion on such matters; but I could not offend you, for I am speaking with friends and for the sake of argument, not in order to criticize. How much better off those princes would have been (God rest their souls) had they tried to equal the ancients in strong and rugged matters instead of delicate and soft ones, in those things done in the heat of the sun and not in the shade, taking their course of action from a true and perfect antiquity, not from that of a false and corrupted one; for when such activities began to please my Romans, my country fell into ruin." To this Cosimo replied—to avoid the inconvenience of having to repeat constantly "he said" and "the other answered,"

8

only the names of the speakers will be noted, without repeating anything else. Therefore:

COSIMO: You have opened the way to an argument that I had hoped for, and I beg you to speak without restraint, since I shall question you without reservations; and if in questioning or responding I excuse or blame anyone, it will not be for the sake of excusing or blaming but to learn the truth from you.

FABRIZIO: And I shall be very happy to tell you what I know about all you ask; as to whether what I say is true or not, I leave that to your judgment. And I shall be very happy if you ask, for I am as ready to learn from your questions as you are from my replies; for a wise interrogator often causes one to reflect upon a number of things and to learn about many others which, without the benefit of questions, one might never have learned.

COSIMO: I'd like to return to what you said first, that my grandfather and those princes of yours would have been wiser to imitate the ancients in manly matters rather than in delicate ones; for I wish to make excuses for my ancestors, leaving excuses for the others to you. I do not believe that there ever was, in his time, a man who detested soft living so much as my grandfather did, or who was ever so fond of that rugged life about which you spoke; nevertheless, he recognized that neither he nor his sons could follow such a life, having been born in a corrupt century where anyone who wished to depart from common customs would be criticized and villified by everyone. For if a man stretched out naked on the sand in the summer under the noonday sun, or upon the snow in the coldest of winter months, as Diogenes did, he would be considered mad. If anyone, like the Spartans, reared his children in the country, making them sleep in the open, go about with their heads uncovered and without shoes, bathe in cold water to induce them to bear up under stress and to make them love life less and to fear death less, he would be ridiculed and considered more of an animal than a man. If anyone, moreover, lived on vegetables and despised gold, as Fabricius Luscinus did, he would be praised by few and followed by none. Therefore, although disgusted by current ways of living, my grandfather abandoned the examples of the ancients in this and followed them only in matters that would attract less attention.

FABRIZIO: You have defended him admirably in this matter, and you certainly speak the truth; but I was not talking so much about such severe ways of life as about other, more humane ways that have more in common with the life of today; these, I believe, would not be difficult for anyone who is counted among a city's leading citizens to introduce. I shall never depart from my Roman friends in recommending examples for anything. If one considers their life and the organization of their republic, one will see that many things there could be introduced into a government that is not totally corrupt.

COSIMO: What are these things that you would like to introduce in imitation of the ancients?

FABRIZIO: To honor and reward ability; not to despise poverty; to value the methods and the institutions of military discipline; to make citizens love one another; to live without factions; to value the public interest over private interests; and other similar principles that could easily suit our times. It is not difficult to be persuaded about these matters when one thinks about them enough and studies them in the correct way, for so much truth can be seen in them that any common intelligence may grasp it. Anyone who institutes such a way of life plants trees under whose shade one can live with greater happiness and prosperity than under this one.

COSIMO: I shall not reply to what you have said in any way (I would rather leave this to the judgment of those who can easily judge it); rather, I shall address myself to you, who accuse those who are not imitators of the ancients in serious and important matters, for I believe that in this manner my intention will be more easily fulfilled. I should like, therefore, to know from you why it is that, on the one hand, you castigate those who do not follow the ancients in their actions while, on the other, in your own art of war, in which you are reputed to be most excellent, you evidently have not made use of any ancient methods or anything similar to those methods.

FABRIZIO: You have landed just where I thought you would, for my remarks deserved no other question, nor did I desire any other one. And although I could save myself with a facile excuse, I would rather, since the time is right, engage in a longer argument for the greater satisfaction of both of us. Men who wish to accomplish an undertaking ought first to prepare themselves with care so that when the opportunity arises they will be able to carry out what they have proposed to do. Since preparations, if they are made carefully, remain unknown, no one can be accused of negligence if his plan is not discovered before that opportunity arises; but when it arrives and he does not act, it becomes obvious that he either did not prepare himself enough or did not have enough foresight. And since I have not yet had the opportunity to be able to demonstrate the preparations I have drawn up to lead military arts back to their ancient institutions, if I have not led them back I cannot be criticized either by you or by others. I believe that this excuse should suffice as a reply to your accusation.

COSIMO: It would more than suffice if I were certain that the opportunity had not arisen.

FABRIZIO: But since you question whether or not this opportunity has arisen, I wish, if you will bear with me, to discuss at length what kind of preparations should be made first, what sort of opportunity must arise, and which difficulties keep the preparations from working and the opportunity from arising. This matter is both very difficult and extremely easy to accomplish, although it may seem to be a contradiction.

COSIMO: You could not please me and these others more than by doing this; and if it does not bother you to talk, it will never annoy us to listen to you. But since this discussion must be lengthy, I ask, with your permission, that these friends of mine assist me; we ask only one thing of you: that you will not be irritated if, from time to time, we interrupt you with some important questions.

FABRIZIO: I would be very happy if you, Cosimo, and these other young men question me, for I believe that youth is more amenable to military affairs and is more inclined to believe what I shall say. Older men, with white hair and blood frozen in their veins, are usually partly averse to war and partly beyond correction, for they believe that the times, not defective institutions, force men to live as they do. Therefore, feel free to ask questions of me; I wish you would, not only because it would give me a chance to rest, but also because it pleases me not to leave any doubts in your minds. I'd like to begin with your own words: you told me that in war, my profession, I had not used any of the methods of the ancients. On this topic I maintain that since this is a profession by means of which men cannot live honestly at all times, it cannot be carried on as a profession except in a republic or in a kingdom; neither of these governments, when it is well organized, has ever allowed any of its citizens or subjects to practice it as a profession; nor has any good man ever taken it up as his own particular profession. For a man will never be judged good who, in his work—if he wants to make a steady profit from it—must be rapacious, fraudulent, violent, and exhibit many qualities which, of necessity, do not make him good. Nor can men who practice war as a profession—great men as well as insignificant men—act in any other way, since their profession does not prosper in peacetime. Therefore, such men must either hope for no peace or must profit from times of war in such a manner that they can live off that profit in times of peace. Neither of these thoughts is found in a good man, for the desire to be able to support oneself at all times leads to theft, acts of violence, and the murderous deeds that such soldiers perpetrate on their friends and foes alike. From not desiring peace come the treacherous deeds that military leaders commit against their employers to keep a war going; and if peace does come, it often happens that the leaders, having been deprived of their salary and their living, set up their standards as soldiers of fortune and illegally sack a province without mercy. Do you not remember, in your own affairs, how countless numbers of soldiers, finding themselves unemployed in Italy after the end of the wars, joined together in many brigades, which were called companies, and went about holding up towns for ransom and sacking the countryside, and no one was able to find a remedy? Have you not read that the Carthaginian soldiers, at the end of the first war with the Romans—under Matho and Spendius (two leaders chosen by them from the mob)—waged a more dangerous war against the Carthaginians than they had just finished waging against the Romans? In the times of our fathers, Francesco Sforza, in order to live honorably in

14

times of peace, not only tricked the Milanese who hired him but also took away their liberty and became their prince. All the other professional soldiers of Italy have been like him; and if they have not, through their evil deeds, become dukes of Milan, they deserve to be blamed even more, for without so much profit they all have the same drawbacks as he—this is evident if one examines their lives. Sforza, the father of Francesco, forced Queen Giovanna of Naples to throw herself into the arms of the King of Aragon when he abandoned her suddenly and left her unarmed in the midst of her enemies, his only purpose being to satisfy his ambition and to extort money from her or to take the kingdom away from her. Andrea Braccio da Montone sought to occupy the Kingdom of Naples by the same means; had he not been routed and slain at Aquila, he would have succeeded. Similar disorders are born from no other reason except that there have been men who used the trade of a soldier as their profession. Do you not have a proverb that reinforces my arguments? "War produces thieves and peace hangs them." For those who do not know how to live by another means and cannot find anyone who will hire them, not having enough ability to join together to commit an honorable act of evil, are forced by necessity to become highway robbers, and justice is forced to execute them.

COSIMO: You have made this military profession of yours seem worthless, and I had thought it to be the most excellent and the most honorable profession there was. Therefore, if you do not explain yourself better, I shall remain unsatisfied, for if what you say is true, I do not know from whence arises the glory of Caesar, Pompey, Scipio, Marcellus, and so many other Roman leaders who are celebrated as gods.

FABRIZIO: I have not yet finished what I proposed to say regarding two matters: first, that a good man cannot make this trade his profession; second, that a republic or a kingdom that is well organized has never permitted her subjects or citizens to make it their profession. Concerning the first statement, I have said all that has come to my mind. There remains the second, and with it I shall respond to your last question. Let me say that Pompey, Caesar, and practically all those leaders after the last Carthaginian war acquired fame as brave men, not as good ones; and those who lived before them acquired glory as both brave and good men. This came about because the latter did not take up the exercise of war as their profession, while the former did make it their profession. While the republic thrived in an uncorrupted state, no great citizen ever presumed, by such a means, to increase his power during peacetime, to break the laws, despoil the provinces, usurp and tyrannize his country or in any manner to increase his station; nor did anyone of low rank think of violating his oath, entering into private conspiracies, not fearing the senate, or perpetrating some tyrannical injury in order to be able to live at all times by means of the art of war. Those who were leaders, content with their triumphs, returned willingly to private life; and those who were regular soldiers laid down their arms more willingly than they had taken them up; and each man returned to the profession that had earned him his living before; nor was there anyone who hoped to make his living by plundering or by means of a military profession. One thinks, when talking about great citizens, of the obvious case of Regulus Atilius, captain of the Roman armies in Africa, who, after nearly defeating the Carthaginians, demanded permission from the senate to return home in order to take care of his lands, which had been ruined by his workers. Now, it is clearer than the sun that if that man had practiced war as his profession, and had thought to make a profit by means of it, having in his grasp so many provinces, he would never have asked permission to return home to care for his fields; for on any one day he could have made much more money than the total worth of all his lands.

But since these good men, who did not practice war as their profession, did not wish to gain anything from it but toil, dangers, and glory, when they had become renowned enough they only wanted to return to their homes and to their professions. And as for men of lower estate and common soldiers, it is clear that they followed the same practice, for each of them gladly left such an occupation; when he was not fighting, he was willing to do so, and when he was fighting, he wanted not to fight. This can be proved in a number of ways, particularly when we observe how among the major privileges the Roman people bestowed upon its citizens was that of not being forced, against one's will, to become a soldier. As long as she was well organized (which she was until the time of the Gracchi), Rome did not have a single soldier who assumed that duty as a profession; because of this she had few bad soldiers, and those who were bad were severely punished. Therefore, a well-organized city must desire that this study of warfare be pursued as an exercise in peacetime and as a necessity and for glory in wartime; it must allow only its citizens to practice it as a profession, as Rome did. And any citizen who, in practicing this profession, does so with another purpose in mind, is not a good citizen; and any city that is governed otherwise is not well organized.

COSIMO: I am very pleased and satisfied with what you have said until now, and this conclusion which you have drawn pleases me as well; as far as a republic is concerned, I believe that your opinion is correct, but as far as kings are concerned, I am uncertain, for I would suppose that a king might wish to have around him men who would make just such a pursuit their profession.

FABRIZIO: A well-instituted kingdom should avoid such professional soldiers even more, since they alone are the source of the corruption of its king and, in sum, the ministers of tyranny. And do not cite as a contrary example any present kingdom, for I shall deny that those are well-organized kingdoms. Kingdoms that have good institutions do not give absolute authority to their kings except in the command of their armies; for only in this institution are sudden decisions necessary; because of this, a single individual must be in charge. In other matters the king cannot do anything without advice, and his advisers would have to live in fear that he has around him in times of peace those who desire war, for they make their living from it.

But I want to consider this question at greater length. I do not wish to select a kingdom that is completely good but one that is like some we have today, where those who practice war as their profession are still to be feared by kings. Since the nerve of any army, without question, lies in the infantry, if a king does not arrange things in such a way that his infantrymen are content to return home and to live off their trades during times of peace, he will of necessity come to ruin; for there exists no more dangerous sort of infantry than one composed of men who make war their profession, since you are forced either to make war constantly and repeatedly pay these men, or run the risk that they will take your kingdom from you. To wage war constantly is not possible; one cannot pay them repeatedly either; therefore, of necessity one runs the risk of losing the state.

As I have mentioned, as long as my Roman friends were wise and good, they never permitted their citizens to choose this activity as their profession, notwithstanding the fact that they would have been able to employ them continuously since they constantly made war. But in order to avoid the dangers that can arise from the continuous practice of war, they varied the men, since the circumstances did not vary, and acted in such a fashion that every fifteen years they rotated the ranks of their legions; thus, they took advantage of men in their prime, which lasts from eighteen to thirty-five years of age, during which time their legs, hands, and eyes are in perfect accord; nor did they wait until their strength grew weaker and their maliciousness grew stronger, as they did later during corrupt times. For first Octavian, and after him Tiberius—both of whom were concerned more for personal power than for the public welfare—began to disarm the Roman people in order to be able to command more easily and to keep those same armies at the frontiers of the empire. And since they thought that such measures as these would not be sufficient to keep the people and the Roman senate in check, they instituted another army, called the Praetorian Guard, which stayed close to the walls of the city and turned it into a stronghold. And because they allowed the men who were selected for this army to make it their profession, these men immediately became insolent and posed a threat to the senate as well as a danger to the emperor. As a result of the guards' unruly nature many emperors were put to death, for these men could give the empire to, or take it from, whomever they chose; and sometimes it would happen that a number of emperors were created by various armies at the same time. These things first led to the division of the empire and finally to its ruin. Therefore, if kings want to live securely, they must be sure that their foot soldiers are made up of men who go to war of their own accord and, when the time comes, return home when peace arrives even more willingly than when they left. This will always occur when the king chooses men who know how to live better by any profession other than a military one. Thus, he must want his subordinates to come back to rule their own people when peace returns, his gentlemen to return to the administration of their properties, and his foot soldiers to return to their own particular trades; and each of these groups will willingly wage war in order to have peace and will not seek to disturb the peace in order to wage war.

COSIMO: This argument of yours truly appears to be well founded; nevertheless, since it is almost the contrary of what I thought until now, my mind is still not purged of every doubt; for I see how many lords and gentlemen live during peacetime by means of the military profession, like yourself, who are hired by princes and by cities. I also see that almost all these professional soldiers regularly receive their wages; I see many foot soldiers still guarding cities and fortresses—and it would appear to me that there is ample employment for everyone in time of peace.

FABRIZIO: I do not think that you believe that every man has his own position during peacetime; for, assuming that no other reason can be put forward, the small number of those troops who remain in those places you mentioned would respond to you. What proportion of the foot soldiers needed in wartime are necessary in peacetime? For fortresses and cities which are guarded in peacetime are guarded even more in time of war; and to them are added the soldiers who are kept in the field, whose numbers are numerous and who are disbanded in peacetime. And concerning garrisons of states (which are small in number), Pope Julius and you Florentines have demonstrated to everyone how much those who only know how to practice the profession of war are to be feared; you have thrown such men out of your guards and have replaced them with Swiss men, since the latter were born and raised in obedience to the law and were selected by their communities by means of an honest election. So, from now on you should not maintain that there is employment for every man in peacetime. As for horsemen, it appears that a solution may be more difficult to find, since they continue to be paid during peacetime. Nevertheless, anyone who carefully considers the whole problem will find the answer easy, for this means of keeping men-at-arms is a corrupt method and is not good. The explanation is that they are men who make a profession of warfare, they would cause a thousand problems every day in the states in which they reside if they were supported by a body of men of sufficient size; but since there are few of them and they are unable to constitute an army by themselves, they are not often able to cause serious damage. Nevertheless, they have done so many times, as I remarked about Francesco

Sforza, his father, and of Braccio da Montone. Therefore, I do not approve of this custom of keeping men-at-arms—it is corrupt and can cause serious problems.

COSIMO: You would do without them? Or, if you kept them, how would you do so?

FABRIZIO: By means of a citizens' militia: not like that of the French king, since it is as dangerous and as arrogant as our own, but like those of the ancients, who created the cavalry from among their own subjects and who, in peacetime, sent them home to live by their own professions, as I shall explain in more detail before this argument is ended. If this sector of the army can live from such activity during peacetime, this is the result of a corrupt institution. As for the appropriations reserved for myself and other military leaders, I say that this, in like manner, is a very corrupt institution; for a wise republic must not grant this to anyone; on the contrary, it must use its own citizens as its military leaders in wartime and must want them to return to their professions in peacetime. Likewise, a wise king ought not to pay such salaries or, if he does pay them, he should do so either as a reward for some distinguished deed or in order to assure himself of the services of a man both in peacetime and in wartime.

And since you cite my own case, I want to use myself as an illustration: I maintain that I have never followed war as a profession, since my profession is to govern my subjects and to defend them, and, in order to defend them, to love peace and to know how to wage war. My king rewards and esteems me not so much for my knowledge about warfare as for my advice during peacetime. No king, therefore, if he is wise and wishes to rule prudently, should want to have around him anyone who is not of the same feelings; for if he has around him either too many lovers of peace or too many lovers of war, they will make him err. According to my proposals here in my first discourse, I cannot speak further on this matter; and if what I have said does not suffice, you should seek someone else to satisfy you further. You can well begin to understand what difficulties there are in bringing ancient methods back into present wars and what preparations a wise man must make, and what opportunities one must hope for, in order to bring such plans to fulfillment; but you will gradually come to understand these matters better, if my argument does not tire you, when you compare any part of ancient institutions to modern methods.

COSIMO: If we wished, at the outset, to hear you discuss such matters, what you have said about them up to this moment has truly doubled our wishes; therefore, we thank you for what we have received and we beg you for the rest.

FABRIZIO: Since this pleases you, I wish to treat this subject from the beginning so that you may understand it better, for it is possible in this way to explain more completely. The goal of anyone wishing to wage war is to be able to do battle with any enemy in the field and to be able to win the day. To wish to do so necessitates the institution of an army. To institute the army, it is necessary to find men, arm them, organize them, drill them in both small and large groups, quarter them, and confront the enemy with them, either marching or taking up a fixed position. In these matters resides all the labor of a field campaign, the most necessary and most honorable kind. For anyone who understands how to draw up his troops for battle, and other errors he may commit in conducting the war will be tolerable; but anyone who lacks this discipline, even if he excels in in other particulars, will never conduct a war with honor, for winning one battle cancels out all of your other mistaken actions; thus, in the same manner, all of the good works you previously accomplished are useless when a battle is lost.

Since men must first be found, however, it is necessary to come to the matter of conscription of soldiers, which the ancients called the *delectus*. We refer to it as the draft, but in order to call it by a more honorable title, I should like to retain the name of conscription. Those who set up rules for warfare wanted the men to be selected from temperate climates, so that they would possess both spirit and prudence; for a warm climate produces prudent but less courageous men, while a cold climate produces brave but foolhardy men. This rule is very useful for a prince who governs many lands, for he is permitted to choose his men from the places that will best serve him; but, in order to provide a rule on this topic that will be of use to anyone, it is necessary to state that every republic and every kingdom must select troops from its own territories, either hot, cold, or temperate. For we witness from ancient examples how in every country with an army one can produce good soldiers; for where natural talent is lacking, perseverance (a quality that, in this instance, is more valuable than natural talent) can provide a remedy. Choosing them from other places cannot be called conscription, since this means taking the best from a province and having the authority to select those who are unwilling to serve as well as those who are willing to serve. One cannot, however, make such a choice except in regions under one's own rule, since you cannot force those who are not in your own domain to serve you.

COSIMO: And it is still possible, from among those who wish to volunteer, to choose some and to reject others; and because of this it can still be called conscription.

FABRIZIO: You are correct to a certain extent, but consider the defects inherent in conscription, since many times it is not even conscription at all. The first problem: those who are not your subjects and who serve as volunteers are not the best; on the contrary, they are the worst soldiers of a province. For if there are any men who are scandalous, lazy, uncontrollable, atheists, fugitives from paternal authority, swearers, gamblers, or poorly bred, they are those who wish to serve in the army. Their customs cannot be more contrary to a true and good militia. When so many of these men offer themselves to you that you can choose more than you need, you may select them; but with such poor material, it is not likely that this type of conscription will be of any use. But in many instances there are insufficient numbers of men to meet your needs, so that you are forced to take them all; for this reason you cannot call this a conscription but rather a hiring of soldiers. Today, by means of this poor system, all of the armies of Italy and elsewhere are being formed, except for Germany, for no one there is taken on by the prince's orders, but only according to the wish of whoever volunteers to serve as a soldier. Consider for yourselves, then, which methods of those ancient armies can be introduced into an army of men assembled in such a fashion.

COSIMO: What method would you employ, then, to raise an army?

FABRIZIO: The one I mentioned: select them from the prince's subjects and with his authority.

COSIMO: Among those selected in this fashion, could you introduce any ancient procedures?

FABRIZIO: Of course, if he who commanded them were their prince or their established lord in a principality; or if he were a citizen and temporarily a captain in a republic; otherwise it is difficult to accomplish anything of value.

COSIMO: Why?

FABRIZIO: I shall explain this in time; now let it suffice for me to say that it is not possible to operate in any other way.

COSIMO: Since, therefore, this conscription must be made

in one's own territories, where do you deem it best to choose your men, from the cities or from the countryside?

FABRIZIO: Those who have written about this problem are all in agreement that it is best to choose them from the countryside, since they are men used to hardships, brought up in toil, accustomed to being in the sun and to avoiding the shade; they are men who can use tools, dig ditches, carry burdens, and who are without guile and without malice. But in this regard, my opinion would be that since soldiers are of two kinds, infantrymen and cavalry, one should select infantrymen from the countryside and cavalry from the towns.

COSIMO: At what age would you take them?

FABRIZIO: If I had to create a new militia, I would choose my men from seventeen to forty years of age; if the militia were already established and I had to renew it, I would always take them at seventeen.

COSIMO: I do not fully understand this distinction.

FABRIZIO: I shall explain it to you. If I had to institute a militia where there was none, it would be necessary to select all those men who were most qualified, provided that they be of military age, in order to train them in the manner I shall shortly explain; but if I had to make a selection in places where this militia was already instituted, I would take men of seventeen as supplementary soldiers, for the older men would already be chosen and in service.

COSIMO: Therefore, you would want to establish a citizen's militia similar to that which we have here.

FABRIZIO: That is correct. But I would arm them, set up their leaders, train and organize them in a manner which I am not sure you follow here.

COSIMO: You are then praising the citizens' militia?

FABRIZIO: Why would you wish me to condemn it?

COSIMO: Because many wise men have always criticized it.

FABRIZIO: You contradict yourself when you say that a wise man criticizes the militia; while such a man may be reputed wise, he can easily be otherwise.

COSIMO: The poor showing it has always made will force us to retain such an opinion.

FABRIZIO: Be careful that the shortcoming is not yours rather than the militia's, as you will come to realize before this discussion is finished.

COSIMO: If you can convince us of this, you will be doing a very good thing; yet I wish to tell you why others criticize it in order that you may justify yourself better. They say this: that it will either be useless—in which case to trust in the militia will cause us to lose the state—or it will be effective—in which case whoever commands the militia will easily be able to take the state from us. The Romans are cited as examples of people who, using these kinds of soldiers, lost their liberty. The Venetians and the King of France are cited: the former used the arms of others in order to prevent any of their own citizens from seizing power, while the king disarmed his own people in order to be able to govern them more easily. But they fear its inefficacy more than this. They cite two principal reasons for this inefficacy: first, that the soldiers are inexperienced; second, that the men are forced to serve as soldiers. They claim that men seldom learn anything and that force never does any good.

FABRIZIO: All these reasons you mention are put forward by shortsighted men, as I shall clearly demonstrate to you. First, as for the inefficacy of the militia, I say to you that no militia can be more efficacious than your own, nor can anyone's own militia be organized except in this manner. And because this allows no room for argument, I do not wish to lose time dwelling on it—let all of the examples from ancient history be sufficient. And since they cite inexperience and force, I say that it is true that inexperience produces fear and that force produces discontent; but courage and experience can be instilled in them by arming, drilling, and organizing them, as you will see in the course of this argument. But, as for force, you have to understand that the men who are brought into the militia by order of the prince have to enter neither under force nor completely voluntarily. For if they were all volunteers, the inconveniences I mentioned above would arise; that is, there would not be a conscription and there would be few who would go. In like manner, compulsion would bring about bad results. Therefore, one must choose a middle path where neither compulsion nor free will is the sole operative, but where the men are attracted by a respect they have for the prince and where they fear his anger more than their immediate inconvenience. And it always turns out to be a force formed by means of free will in such a way that no discontent, which might lead to bad effects, will come of it. I do not, however, because of this, say that it cannot be defeated, for the Roman armies were defeated many times and the army of Hannibal was beaten; it is clear that no one can organize an invincible army. However, these wise men of yours must not measure the inefficacy of this sort of army by a single defeat; they should believe that just as it can be defeated, it can similarly conquer and remedy the cause of its defeat. And when they search for this remedy, they will discover that it will not have resulted from a defect in method but rather from the imperfection of its organization. And, as I said, they ought to make provisions for this, not by accusing the citizens' militia but by correcting it. You will learn how this must be done as we go along.

As for your fears that such an institution may deprive you of your state by means of the individual who becomes its captain, I reply that arms carried by one's citizens or subjects, when they are bestowed by law and are well organized, never do harm; on the contrary, they are always useful, and cities are maintained without corruption by means of them better than they are without them. Rome remained free for four hundred years and was armed; Sparta, for eight hundred; many other cities were unarmed and remained free for less than forty years. Cities need military forces, and when they do not have their own they hire foreigners. These foreign soldiers are more likely to harm the public good than are one's own men, since such men are more easily corrupted and more likely to be used by some citizen seeking power; such a man has easier material to manage, since he wishes to oppress men who are unarmed. Besides this, a city will fear two enemies more than one. A city that uses foreign troops simultaneously fears the foreigner it hires as well as the citizen. To prove that this fear does exist, let me remind you of what I said earlier concerning Francesco Sforza. A city that uses its own troops fears only its own citizens. In spite of the many reasons I can bring to bear, I would have this one suffice: no one ever established a republic or a kingdom who did not believe that the same people who lived there would also defend it with their arms.

And if the Venetians had been as wise in this matter as in their other institutions, they could have set up a new monarchy in the world. They deserve even more blame since they had been armed by their first lawgivers. Not possessing any territory on land, they were armed at sea, where they carried out their wars with great skill and, through their own arms, increased their homeland. But when the time came for them to wage war on the mainland in order to defend Vicenza, instead of sending one of their citizens to fight on land they hired the Marquis of Mantua as their leader. This was the unfortunate policy that cut off their legs and kept them from climbing to Heaven's greatness. And if they did this out of the belief that they knew how to fight at sea but were unsure as to how to do so on land, this was an unwise move; for a sea captain, experienced in fighting the winds, the waters, and men, can become a leader on land more easily than a captain on land can become a sea captain. My Roman friends, knowing how to fight on land but not on the sea, did not hire Greeks or Spaniards familiar with the sea when they fought the Carthaginians, who were powerful on the ocean; rather, they imposed that duty on the citizens they usually used to fight on land—and they triumphed. If the Venetians hired foreign soldiers lest one of their citizens could become a tyrant, this was a senseless fear; for, besides the arguments on this matter that I advanced a while ago, if a citizen with naval forces had never made himself a tyrant in a city situated on the sea, he would have had even less chance with ground forces. If they had considered this, they would have seen that it is not arms in the hands of one's citizens that produce tyrants but rather the evil institutions of the government that tyrannize a city; and if a city has a good government, it need not fear its armies. Therefore, they chose an imprudent policy which caused them to lose much glory and much peace of mind. As for the error the King of France committed in not keeping his own people disciplined in warfare (a case those citizens of yours cite as an example), no one who sets aside his own private feelings will judge that this is not a defect in that kingdom and not the sole cause of its weakness.

But I have made too great a digression, and perhaps I

have strayed from my topic; yet I have done so in order to reply to you and to show you that one cannot build one's foundation on forces other than one's own, and one cannot organize one's own forces in any fashion other than by means of a citizens' militia, nor can one introduce other kinds of armies or military discipline by any other means. If you have read about the institutions established by the first kings in Rome, especially by Servius Tullius, you will discover that the organization of the classes was nothing other than a regulation permitting the quick assembly of an army for the defense of the city. But let us return to conscription. I repeat, if I had to recruit for an existing army, I should pick men of seventeen; but if I had to create a new one, I should choose men between the ages of seventeen and forty in order to be able to make use of them immediately.

COSIMO: Would you distinguish among the professions of the men you select?

FABRIZIO: These writers I have cited do so, for they do not wish us to choose fowlers, fishermen, cooks, whoremongers, and anyone who makes a profession of pleasure; they suggest, rather, that we select farmers, blacksmiths, farriers, carpenters, butchers, hunters, and other similar trades. But I would make very little distinction between men and their quality based upon their professions, although I would do so regarding their usefulness. Peasants who are accustomed to working the fields are more useful than anyone, since of all trades this is the most frequently used in the army. After them come blacksmiths, carpenters, farriers, and stonemasons, of whom it is useful to have a great many, since their trades serve in many areas; it is always a good thing to have a soldier from whom you can require double service.

Book II

COSIMO: I should like to learn from you, if you have pondered the matter, how it is that so much cowardice, so much lack of order, and so much neglect of these military matters exist in our times?

FABRIZIO: I shall gladly tell you what I think about the matter. You know that although there have been many famous warriors in Europe, there have been few in Africa and even fewer in Asia. This comes about because these last two regions of the world have had only one or two principalities and few republics; Europe alone has had several kingdoms and countless republics. Men become excellent and demonstrate their ability to the extent that they are employed and are advanced by their prince, their republic, or their king; therefore, it follows that where there are many rulers, there are many valiant men; and where there are few rulers, these men are few in number. In Asia one finds Ninus, Cyrus, Artaxerxes, Mithridates—very few others are fit to be in their company. In Africa, leaving aside the ancient Egyptians, we can name Masinissa, Jugurtha, and the leaders produced by the Carthaginian republic; when compared with those of Europe, however, these are few, for in Europe there are countless excellent men, and there would be many more if, together with those already known, we could name the others who are lost to us because of the malevolence of time. For the world has been more distinguished in those areas where the existing states have favored ability, either because of necessity or because of some human characteristic. In Asia, then, there arose few such men since that region was completely under a single kingdom, which, because of its size, remained listless for much of the time; it could not produce men distinguished in what they do. In Africa the same thing occurred; yet more great men were produced there because of the Carthaginian republic. For more great men spring from republics than from kingdoms, since in republics ability is usually revered while in kingdoms it is feared, so it is that in republics great men are encouraged while in kingdoms they are destroyed.

Anyone who examines Europe will find it to be full of republics and principalities which, out of the fear they have for each other, are obliged to keep alive their military institutions and to honor those who had distinguished themselves in service. In Greece, besides the kingdom of the Macedonians, there were many republics, and in each of them very great men rose up. In Italy there were the Romans, the Samnites, the Tuscans, and the Cisalpine Gauls. France and Germany were full of republics and princes, as was Spain. And although in comparison to the Romans few other men of this caliber are named, this is the result of malicious historians who follow Fortune and usually limit themselves to praise of the victors. It is not reasonable to suppose that among the Samnites and the Tuscans, who fought 150 years with the Roman people before being subdued, there did not exist a great number of excellent men. And the same is true for France and Spain. But that ability which historians do not praise in individual men they praise in a general way in their race, when they exalt to the stars the obstinacy that such people displayed in defending their freedom.

Since it is therefore true that where there are more states there are more able men, it must follow that if these states are done away with, their ability is likewise done away with, for what has produced the able men has been removed. Therefore, when the Roman empire later grew and destroyed all of the republics and the principalities of Europe and Africa and, for the most part, those of Asia, it left no path for ingenuity other than Rome. Then, as time passed, able men became as few in number in Europe as in Asia; and this type of ability reached a final decline when all ability was concentrated in Rome. When Rome was corrupted, almost the entire world came to be corrupted. The Scythian peoples were able to plunder that empire which had destroyed the abilities of others without knowing how to maintain its own. Even though that empire, as a result of the flood of these barbarians, was subsequently divided into many parts, this ability was not reborn there. One explanation for this is that it is a difficult matter to restore institutions after they have been destroyed. Another is that the manner of living today, as a consequence of the Christian religion, does not force one to defend oneself as it did in ancient times. For then men defeated in war were either killed or sold into perpetual slavery, where they led miserable lives; captured territories were either devastated or their inhabitants were driven out; their possessions were seized and they were scattered all over the world, so that those who were overcome in warfare suffered every form of misery. Terrorized by this fear, men kept military training alive and honored those who excelled in it.

But today this fear has, for the most part, been lost; few defeated men are killed and none are kept prisoner for a long time, for they can easily free themselves. Cities, even when they rebel a thousand times, are not leveled. Men are permitted to keep their property, so that the worst evil one fears is a tax. Men therefore do not wish to submit themselves to military institutions and to exert themselves therein in order to avoid those dangers that they do not actually fear. Furthermore, these European territories are under the rule of very few rulers as compared with the past; for all of France obeys one king, all of Spain obeys another, and Italy has few territories. Weak cities consequently defend themselves by joining anyone who conquers, and powerful states do not fear a complete defeat for the reasons mentioned above.

COSIMO: And yet we have witnessed many cities sacked during the last twenty-five years and some kingdoms lost.

These examples ought to teach others how to live and to revive a number of these ancient institutions.

FABRIZIO: You are correct; but if you will note which towns have been sacked, you will discover that they have not been the capitals of states but less important towns: it was Tortona that was sacked, not Milan; Capua and not Naples; Brescia and not Venice; Ravenna and not Rome. These examples are not enough to make anyone who rules change his policy; on the contrary, they make him more obstinate in the belief that he can buy off his liberty with a ransom; and because of this, such rulers do not wish to submit themselves to the hardships of military training, since they regard such matters as partly unnecessary and partly a matter about which they have no understanding. Those others who are enslaved peoples and to whom such examples ought to instill fear do not have the power to remedy their situation; and those princes who have lost their states have no time to do so; those who still retain them do not understand and have no desire to do so, for they would rely upon Fortune without any inconvenience rather than upon their own ability. They see that Fortune governs everything, since little ability exists there, and they want her to rule them and not them her. And to show that what I say is the truth, just consider Germany, where there are many principalities and republics that contain much ability; all that is good in the military methods of the present day comes from those peoples who, being very jealous of their states and fearing slavery (which is not feared elsewhere), all maintain themselves as free and independent people. I wish this to suffice concerning my opinion on the causes of the present decadence. I do not know if you are in agreement with me or if this discussion has given rise to some doubts.

COSIMO: Not at all! On the contrary! I remain completely convinced.

* * *

Book VII

FABRIZIO: Would you, perhaps, also like to learn what qualities a military captain must possess? I shall be able to satisfy you, and in few words, on that question, for I know of only one man who would know how to accomplish all the things that we have discussed together today; yet the knowledge of these alone would not be sufficient if he did not know how to learn on his own, for no one without inventiveness was ever a great man in his profession; and if invention in other kinds of work honors the man, in this one especially it brings praise. And it is seen that every invention, no matter how insignificant, is celebrated by historians; for it is obvious that they praise Alexander the Great because, in order to break camp more secretively, he did not give the signal by trumpet but with a hat hoisted on a spear. He is also praised for having taught his soldiers to kneel upon the left knee when encountering the enemy in order to withstand their assault more bravely; this new idea not only gave him the victory, it also bestowed upon him such fame that all of the statues erected in his honor were sculpted in that position.

But since it is time to conclude this discussion, I wish to return to my subject, and in so doing I shall escape that penalty usually incurred in this city by those who fail to do so. If you remember, Cosimo, you asked me the reason why I was, on the one hand, an admirer of antiquity and a critic of those who do not imitate it in important matters, and why, on the other hand, I myself did not imitate antiquity in affairs of war which I have made my profession—you could see no reason for this. To this I replied that men who wished to accomplish things should first prepare themselves to learn the art of war in order to be able to put it into operation when the occasion arises. Whether or not I know how to return the militia to its ancient practices I wish you (who have heard me discuss this question at length) to decide. From what I said, I feel certain that you understand how much time I have spent on these thoughts, and you can imagine, I think, how very much I should like to put these thoughts of mine into action. That I have been able to do so, or have even had the opportunity to do so a single time, you can easily determine. To convince you all the more, as well as for my own justification, I now wish to present the reasons. In so doing, I shall partly keep my promise to you by demonstrating how difficult it is, and how easy it could be at this time, to practice the imitation of the ancients. Therefore, let me say that no activity practiced by men today can more easily be brought back to ancient practices than warfare, but it can only be done by those princes who can raise an army, from among the subjects of their state, of between fifteen and twenty thousand young men. On the

44

other hand, nothing is more difficult than this when the prince does not possess this ability.

And in order that you may better understand this part of my argument, you should know that there are two kinds of military leaders who have been praised. One kind includes those leaders who have accomplished great deeds with an army already organized according to its normal discipline; the majority of the Roman citizens and others who have commanded armies are examples of these leaders—men who have not had any other problem except to keep up the training of their men and see that they are well led. Another kind includes those leaders who have not only had to overcome an enemy but who, before reaching that point, were forced to produce a good and well-disciplined army of their own; these men, without a doubt, deserve more praise than those who operated with good and disciplined armies. Examples of this second group of leaders include Pelopidas, Epaminondas, Tullus Hostilius, Philip of Macedonia (the father of Alexander the Great), Cyrus (king of the Persians), and Tiberius Sempronius Gracchus. All these men first had to establish a good army and then wage war with it. They were all able to accomplish this, both because of their wisdom and because they had subjects fit to receive such training. It would never have been possible for one of them, however great his ability, to accomplish such a praiseworthy deed if he had been a mercenary in a foreign country, full of corrupt men unaccustomed to any sort of honorable obedience.

Therefore, in Italy it is not enough to know how to command a previously established army; it is first necessary to know how to create one, and then how to command it. And to do this there must be princes who, possessing much territory and many subjects, have the capacity to do so. I cannot be counted among these, for I have never commanded, nor can I command, unless it is in an army of foreigners and men obligated to others than myself; whether or not it is possible to introduce among such men some of the things we discussed today I leave to your judgment. How can I make one of these soldiers who bears arms today carry more arms than he usually does; and, in addition to his arms, rations for two or three days and a shovel? How can I make him dig or keep him every day, and for many hours, practicing drills so that I can use him in real battles? How will he keep himself from gambling, whoring, swearing, and from the general insubordination of today's army? How can he be brought back to such a degree of discipline, obedience, and respect that a tree full of apples in the middle of the camp would remain untouched? We have read how many times this occurred in ancient armies. What can I promise them that will make them fear me or respect me if, after the war, they know they will have nothing further to do with me? How can I make them feel shame when they are born and raised without it? Why should they obey me when they do not know me? By what God or saints should I have them swear: by those they worship or by those they curse? The saints they worship I do not know, but I certainly know the ones they curse. How can I believe that they will keep the promises they made to those they continuously despise? How can those who have contempt for God honor men? What good form, therefore, could possibly be stamped on this raw material?

And if you tell me that the Swiss and the Spanish are good soldiers, I will confess to you that they are a good deal better than the Italians; but if you pay attention to my argument and the practice of these two peoples, you will see how they both lack many things required to attain the perfection of the ancients. The Swiss became good soldiers as a result of one of their customs, which I described to you today, while the others were made good out of necessity. Waging war in a foreign land and believing themselves to be faced with a choice of either victory or death, the Spanish became good soldiers because they had no place to flee. But it is a goodness defective in many parts, for the only good thing in it is their common practice of meeting the enemy with the point of their pike or sword. Nor is there anyone capable of teaching them what they lack—even less, one who does not speak their language.

But let us return to the Italians, who, in not having wise princes, have not accepted any good institutions; and because they have not experienced the necessity that the Spanish felt, they have not adopted any for themselves.

They therefore are scorned by the rest of the world. It is not the people who are to blame, but rather their princes, who have been punished and who, because of their ignorance, have received the fitting penalty of losing their states ignominiously and without having done a single admirable deed. Do you wish to test whether what I have said is true? Consider, then, how many wars have been fought in Italy since the invasion of King Charles VIII until the present day. Although wars usually make men warlike and renowned, the longer and more savage these wars were, the more they caused a loss of reputation, both of the subjects and their rulers. This came about because the traditional institutions were not, and are still not, good; and there is no one here who has known how to adopt any new institutions. Nor should you ever believe that a reputation can be won for Italian arms except through the means that I have enumerated and through the deeds of those who possess the greatest states in Italy; for this form can only be stamped upon simple, rough, and independent men, not upon evil, badly governed, and foreign ones. Nor has any good sculptor ever been found who believes that he can make as beautiful a statue from a piece of poorly blocked marble as he can from one that is rough.

Before they had felt the blows of the Transalpine wars, our Italian princes believed that a prince need only know how to dream up witty replies in his study; write a beautiful letter; display intelligence and readiness in his conversation and his speech; weave a fraud; adorn himself with gems and gold; sleep and eat in a more splendid style than others; surround himself with a large number of courtesans; conduct himself in a miserly and arrogant manner with his subjects; rot in laziness; give military positions as favors; despise anyone who had shown them any praiseworthy path; and expect that their pronouncements be taken as oracles. Nor did these wretched men realize that they were preparing themselves to become the prey of anyone who assaulted them. This resulted in the great terrors, the sudden flights, and the miraculous losses of 1494; thus, three very powerful states of Italy were sacked and despoiled many times. But what is worse is that those princes who still remain persist in the same errors and live in the same disorder; they do not consider that those who, in ancient times, wished to maintain their states did, and had done, all of the things that I have discussed—their goal was to prepare the body for hardships and the mind not to fear danger. Thus it came about that Caesar, Alexander, and all those excellent men and princes were foremost in their soldiers' ranks and went about in armor on foot; they would rather lose their lives than their states; in such a manner they lived and died valiantly. One could, perhaps, condemn some of them for being overambitious for power, but one could never accuse any of them of being too soft or of any other characteristic that makes a man delicate and unwarlike. If these things were read and believed by Italian princes, it would be impossible for them not to bring about a change in their way of life and in the fortune of their nations.

And since you complained of your militia in the beginning of our discussion, let me say that if you had organized it as I have explained above, and it had subsequently not proved itself, you would have cause to complain; but if it was not organized and trained in the manner I suggested it could place the blame on you for having produced an abortion instead of a perfect figure. The Venetians, as well as the Duke of Ferrara, tried this method but were unable to carry it through—because of their own defects and not as a result of those of their men. And I can assure you that any of those rulers who possess a state in Italy today and who try this path will be ruler of this province before anyone else. Things will develop in that state as they did in the Kingdom of Macedonia, which, under the rule of Philip—who had learned the manner of organizing armies from Epaminondas the Theban—became so powerful by means of this kind of organization and these practices that it could occupy all of Greece in a few years. While the rest of Greece remained at ease and occupied herself with reciting comedies, Philip left such a foundation to his son that he was able to make himself prince of the entire world.

Therefore, anyone who despises these thoughts despises his principality, if he be a prince; if he be a citizen, he despises his native city. And I complain about Nature, which either should not have made me aware of this or should have given me the means of putting it into practice. Nor can I dream of ever having another opportunity, since I am old; and because of this, I have been very frank with you. Since you are young and qualified, if the things I have said please you, you can, at the proper time and to the profit of your princes, mention them and suggest that they adopt them. I would not have you be afraid or dismayed for this province of Italy, for it seems it was born to revive dead things, as we have seen in its poetry, painting, and sculpture. But as for myself, because I am along in years, I have no hope of seeing this come about. And yet, if Fortune had, in the past, conceded me as great a state as is sufficient for such an enterprise, I believe that I would have shown the world in a very short time how much ancient institutions are worth; and, without a doubt, I would have added to the glory of my state or lost it with no shame.

PENGUIN 60s CLASSICS

PENGUIN 60s CLASSICS

For complete information about books available from Penguin and how to order them, please write to us at the appropriate address below. Please note that for copyright reasons the selection of books varies from country to country.

IN THE UNITED KINGDOM: Please write to *Dept. JC, Penguin Books Ltd, FREEPOST, West Drayton, Middlesex UB7 OBR.*
If you have any difficulty in obtaining a title, please send your order with the correct money, plus ten per cent for postage and packaging, to *PO Box No. 11, West Drayton, Middlesex UB7 OBR.*

IN THE UNITED STATES: Please write to *Consumer Sales, Penguin USA, P.O. Box 999, Dept. 17109, Bergenfield, New Jersey 07621-0120.* VISA and MasterCard holders call 1-800-253-6476 to order all Penguin titles.

IN CANADA: Please write to *Penguin Books Canada Ltd, 10 Alcorn Avenue, Suite 300, Toronto, Ontario M4V 3B2.*

IN AUSTRALIA: Please write to *Penguin Books Australia Ltd, P.O. Box 257, Ringwood, Victoria 3134.*

IN NEW ZEALAND: Please write to *Penguin Books (NZ) Ltd, Private Bag 102902, North Shore Mail Centre, Auckland 10.*

IN INDIA: Please write to *Penguin Books India Pvt Ltd, 706 Eros Apartments, 56 Nehru Place, New Delhi 110 019.*

IN THE NETHERLANDS: Please write to *Penguin Books Netherlands bv, Postbus 3507, NL-1001 AH Amsterdam.*

IN GERMANY: Please write to *Penguin Books Deutschland GmbH, Metzlerstrasse 26, 60594 Frankfurt am Main.*

IN SPAIN: Please write to *Penguin Books S. A., Bravo Murillo 19, 1° B, 28015 Madrid.*

IN ITALY: Please write to *Penguin Italia s.r.l., Via Felice Casati 20, I-20124 Milano.*

IN FRANCE: Please write to *Penguin France S. A., 17 rue Lejeune, F-31000 Toulouse.*

IN JAPAN: Please write to *Penguin Books Japan, Ishikiribashi Building, 2-5-4, Suido, Bunkyo-ku, Tokyo 112.*

IN GREECE: Please write to *Penguin Hellas Ltd, Dimocritou 3, GR-106 71 Athens.*

IN SOUTH AFRICA: Please write to *Longman Penguin Southern Africa (Pty) Ltd, Private Bag X08, Bertsham 2013.*